"5/5 stars - So cute - I have always told stories & played the tickle bear game. All my dogs loved being sung to. They all love that I wind up a music box as that signals it is time to go to sleep. So read this charming book to your dogs it is worth your time." *Starmagic, USA*

"So awesome! I think this book is so cute, and funny, and Bailey here thinks so too, don't u Bailey? Please read this book, u will be happy u did, and so will Fido there, won't u Fido?" *Jenafay Turman, USA*

"At first my mum wasn't very good at reading me these stories but I was genius at listening. I carry the book to her now and stare for Story Time." *Fly, UK*

"My dog Tank and I enjoyed *Bone Dog* most. We recommend it to young dogs and their owners. It shows even pets can share." *Alice Hildebrand, USA*

"5/5 stars I love this book it is my favorite book of the year. *Nancy Erickson, USA*

Stories for My Dog
Published in 2018 by Bibliopet

Eight stories in this collection first published in 2003 by Rodale Press USA as *Tales for Dogs, a* series of four board books: *Glam Dog, City Dog, Bone Dog, Buddy Dog, Silly Dog, Stick Dog, Precious Dog* and *Tricky Dog.*

ISBN-13: 978-1987403213 ISBN-10: 1987403215

www.bibliopet.com

The dog has an enviable mind.
It remembers the nice things in life
and quickly blots out the nasty.

Barbara Woodhouse

- + -

Dogs never lie about love.

Jeffrey Masson

Also by Flora Kennedy

The Wild Folk

Author's Note

People have always read to dogs. It's just a natural progression from talking.

I started telling my first Alaskan Malamute, Boo Boo, stories when we were lazing about one day.

I made them up as I went based on how Boo responded. If he started falling asleep, I stirred him up by saying, "bone!" or "treat". If he was rapt with attention I'd say, "good boy!".

It was a lot of fun. His head-tilts and funny faces made me laugh. It made me feel closer to him, maybe because we were paying close attention to one another for a few minutes.

I noticed that using words he knew - dog, toy, treat, bone, cat and so on piqued his interest.

I also noticed he was tuning-in to my emotions as I told the story; happy, pensive, thoughtful, excited and this seemed satisfying to him.

I wondered, would other dogs and their people have as much fun as we were having? I decided to write stories for dogs based on what I'd learned with Boo.

I've since been reading these stories to Boo and later my second Malamute, Bubba Bear, for years. My daughter found my *Tales for Dogs* books published by Rodale in 2003 on the bookshelf when she was five years old and started reading those stories to Bubba.

The collection of dog stories in *Stories for My Dog* are unabashed, quirky tales written in such a way you'll feel free to make them better and ad-lib them to suit and your dog. Each story takes just a few minutes to read.

The first time you read to them your dog won't know what's going on. But next time they'll remember how good the first time felt and things progress from there.

Having Story Time and making it regular has unexpected rewards. It's funny that no matter how easy we find it to talk to our dog, sometimes we run out of things to say.

There are also those times we can't find the words to say to our beloved dog when, for instance, they might be frightened, injured or not feeling well. Having been in this situation myself, I've written a few stories, like *Sick Dog,* for example, in the hope of supporting you in finding the words you want to say.

Remembering your dog's pleasure at listening to you tell them a story brings memories to cherish in the future. I know because it's that way for me.

And any time your dog is stressed, reading a story that's familiar to them; that they associate with quiet times with you when all was well, can be wonderfully soothing.

For your dog Story Time represents a collection of moments of bliss when they're not expected to do anything at all except bask in feeling deeply connected to you.

I hope you and your dog get as much pleasure, love and fun from *Stories for My Dog* as my dogs and I have enjoyed creating them.

Contents

How do the stories end? With:

Stories for My Dog

Puppy Dog

This story ends with you and your dog playing.

Hey __ (dog's name)! It's story time! Do you want a story? Are you ready?

This is a story about a puppy dog. Being a puppy is fun isn't it __? But it's also the most challenging time of your life. There are so many things to learn, aren't there, __? Yes.

You have to learn about going outside to pee and poop, what's OK to chew and what's not, (this is very hard!) you have to be brave about missing your mom and you have to be clever enough to adapt to all sorts of new experiences. It's exciting, isn't it __?

This particular puppy dog had a very grown up name - he was called Troy, isn't that a good name, __? It's from Greek mythology.

Troy was a Boxer puppy and he liked nothing more than to bounce. Troy bounced whenever he got the chance. Up and down, up and down, up and down just like Tigger who is a tiger in Winnie the Poo stories. And Poo is not a poo but a bear. Gosh, can't words be confusing?

Never mind. Troy's person loved him very much. Even when he was naughty as all puppies can't help being.

But Troy tried so hard to be a good puppy. And his person always said, "My puppy is a good puppy" even when he was not.

Troy had his own bed he could go to which made him feel safe. It was his place where he could relax after training or puppy classes or a walk.

Where do you like to relax __? All right. Troy had lots of things he loved to do. He liked to steal his person's smelly socks and present them to guests.

He liked to crawl under the table and the bed and other tight spaces and nap. He liked to jump all over new friends - dogs and people - to show them how excited he was about meeting them.

He loved to play with his squeaky toys and he loved to chew on the table leg while watching his person intensely. This was not allowed - he'd be given a tug-toy to chew on instead.

Troy had lots of fun adventures. One day, for instance, he met the neighbour's cat. He wanted to be its friend.

This cat stalked him and growled at him and Troy was confused. He sat quietly with a sad look on his face until the cat came towards him and sniffed his nose.

Troy sat very quietly - which is very hard for a puppy to do - and he was rewarded with a cat kiss.

Another day he got to meet a cockatoo that squawked and talked to him like a person. Do you know what a cockatoo is __?

Anyway, Troy also went to the vet and got shots, (and biscuits as well which made him forget about the shots).

Troy had a daily routine and this helped him adapt to all the new things he was learning: breakfast and dinner and a walk. Dogs like routine, don't they __?

Then there were the training sessions that were fun because they didn't last very long and it was Troy's chance to concentrate and be a good boy and get lots of praise.

His person always set Troy up for success so Troy had a good chance of responding correctly.

The best part was the games he'd play

with his person when he could blow off steam by running crazy round the garden. It was so much fun!

Troy's person knew that whatever he put in over Troy's first three years, he'd get back for the rest of his life.

So he learned about patience, just like Troy. Some days he didn't seem to do anything but take things out of Troy's mouth and go see what he was playing with. Living with a puppy can be exhausting!

And Troy's person was especially nervous when Troy was quiet because one time Troy was quiet because he was chewing the sofa! (Yes, it is hard to know what is OK to chew and what isn't – isn't that right __?)

Then came the day that would change everything!

On this day Troy discovered a lot more

new things!

He discovered he couldn't fit under the table or the bed any more and that his own bed was suddenly too small!

He discovered he didn't feel like bouncing so much and he wasn't interested in the table leg. He discovered he wasn't quite so excited about new people; he'd met lots already.

And he didn't even feel like showing off his person's socks any more! What was happening __?

I can tell you. Troy was no longer a puppy - he was a dog! And not just any old dog - he was a magnificent, friendly and good dog. Are you good __? Of course you are! Do you want to play __?

Buddy Dog

This story ends with a hug.

Hey __ (dog's name)! It's story time! Do you want a story __? Are you ready?

I want to tell you about a dog called Buddy. Buddy was a great dog. He could be a pretty naughty dog but he was still great. (And anyways being naughty can be cool too, can't it __ .) Yes.

Are you naughty __? You are great aren't you? Yes. It won't surprise you to know that Buddy got his name because he was such a good friend. We know that dogs can be great pals, don't we __? You are my buddy, aren't you? Uh-huh.

Buddy had lots of friends but his best friend in the whole world wasn't his friend Rolo the Golden Retriever who rumbled with him nor Sasha the Shih Tzu whom he loved to sniff. His best friend was his person, John.

Buddy's person became his best friend

from the moment he saved Buddy's life by springing him out of The Pound. That day was the beginning of a friendship that would change both their lives forever. It turned out that Buddy had learned some bad habits before he met his best friend.

For example, he liked to chew things - it made him feel safe to have soft things in his mouth. He liked to chew blankets and cushions, the bed mattress and even chairs. He couldn't help it. He also couldn't help raiding the garbage can in the kitchen, it was just a leftover habit from the time he was starving on the streets. And there was no way he could resist barking at the neighbor's cat who teased him all the time.

You wouldn't do any of those things would you __? So anyways Buddy and his person went to obedience school. Buddy's person learned he had a lot to learn about dogs while Buddy learned he had a lot of treats to eat. Pretty soon Buddy and his person John could walk on leash together without Buddy pulling John all over the place. You don't do that do you __? You're so smart!

Buddy always had breakfast and dinner and even supper too, and walks at the same time every day. Buddy also got presents like toys that talked to him. For his part, Buddy was always there for his person and always knew when to lean against his person and when to offer a paw.

And he knew so many ways to cheer his person up – like bringing his person a toy to play with or the newspaper from the front porch or un-digging a particularly smelly bone he'd buried months before and putting it under his person's pillow. He's probably right now carrying this same book we've got here to his person for Story Time.

One day when Buddy and John were out walking, Buddy stopped and looked behind him. (This was just a thing he did so as not to miss out on half of life.)

John also stopped and looked behind. Oh, no! A huge, angry dog was coming towards them! It was obvious he was looking for a fight! John shouted at the strange dog as loud as he could. The dog stopped in his tracks but then he bared his teeth and raised his hackles.

Buddy held his ground. He wasn't going to let some bad dog threaten him or his person even if he was a scary-looking dog.

Suddenly a loud crash scared all of them and - phew __! - the strange dog ran away.

On the sidewalk were the remains of a pot plant and when Buddy and John looked up to see where it had come from they saw a woman waving and a dog smiling at them from a second storey window.

Buddy barked and let his tongue hang out. The woman gestured for them to come up. Would you believe __ that Buddy pulled John up all those stairs? He did.

The thing is that even an obedience-trained dog like Buddy is a friend first and foremost isn't that right __. And unlike his not-so-good-at-scenting person, Buddy could smell love in the air. Come here and let's have a hug. Do you want a hug __?

Silly Dog

This story ends with a cuddle.

Hey __ (dog's name)! It's story time! Do you want a story __? Are you ready?

This is a story about a silly dog. This dog was so silly he didn't know a bone from a cat's bottom. He would get wildly excited when the wind blew a new smell over the fence and over his nose!

One day, he smelled something truly amazing. He didn't know what it was but it smelled so good! He'd never smelled anything like it, ever.

It was the smell of fresh mountain streams and an old sheep's carcass, mixed with some fresh poo and something like chocolate. Yes, you know what that is don't you? But you can't have any chocolate because it's poisonous! __ are you listening, that's important information. Of course you are because you're such a good dog! Yes!

Do you want to know what happened to this silly dog, __? After smelling the most fantastic smell he'd ever smelled, he peeped through a hole in the fence and saw two dogs playing together in the park nearby.

He knew it was dangerous to leave his yard but he was a silly dog so he did a silly thing. He escaped! Yes, he did!

He didn't know quite how it happened. One minute he was jumping up and down and barking on the spot and the next he was in the air and over the fence. He wanted so much to play with the other dogs – but they ran away!

They had longer legs than him so they disappeared faster than a rabbit. This dog, who was not as clever as you, __, stood in the street and realized he didn't know where he was. All the smells were different. He was afraid. Have you ever been afraid __?

Suddenly a big truck approached. Out of it jumped a man carrying a long pole with a noose. And do you know what happened, __?

The man lassoed this poor, silly dog and bundled him into the back of the truck. This dog felt very silly, indeed.

He had to spend all day with two big black dogs who snarled at him.

Worse - the smells in the kennel were terrible: smells of hundreds of unhappy dogs and yucky things like disinfectant. It was horrible! Silly Dog had been captured and put in The Pound!

Fortunately, even though he was a silly dog, he had very clever people. They phoned all the local vets and the local police and the ASPCA to see if anyone had seen their silly dog. They found their silly dog right away and took him home that night.

This silly dog went straight to his bed, crept under his blanket and was too scared to move!

Until the smell of sausages cooking in garlic came wafting over his nose from the kitchen.

Of course he had to go and investigate. So you see, __ this is why we love you even though you can be a silly dog sometimes: you are a dog and we love the doggy things you do __. Do you want a cuddle __?

Farm Dog

This story ends with your dog winning a prize, (a treat or new toy or perhaps a rosette).

Hey __ (dog's name)! It's story time! Do you want a story __? Are you ready?

This is a story about a farm dog. His name was Jake and he'd lived all his long life on the farm. He worked for his food and shelter - he was a sheepdog.

If there was one thing Jake loved to do it was chase things. It didn't matter what he was chasing. He'd chase the quadbike, the tractor, the chickens, the cats, the children - he'd even chase the leaves that fell on his head. But he was best at chasing the sheep.

He liked the sheep because they always did as they were told, like Jake always did as he was told. "Get back!" "Come round!" "In behind!" "Stop!" "On by!" Jake knew lots of commands.

Sometimes he knew better than the farmer and the farmer would shout angrily at him and blow his whistle, but Jake was always one step ahead. Are you listening __? Good.

One day Jake realized he wasn't running quite so fast as he usually did. It wasn't that he'd pulled a muscle or anything like that - he was too fit for that nonsense __.

His son, Dirk, ran faster than he did and even overtook him. Dirk headed off the ewe and her lamb who had strayed. (You don't stray do you __? Good dog!)

Being in charge of straying sheep was Jake's job. He wondered if the farmer had noticed what Dirk had done. He had. When they got back to the farm at sunset, the farmer rubbed his hand up and down Jake's leg, "It's a bit swollen there, old fella" said the farmer.

The farmer's wife stroked his leg gently and Jake wagged his tail slowly while they checked him out. “Maybe a touch of arthritis, Jake. You won’t be going up the hill with us tomorrow, nor the next” said the farmer.

“It might be time for a permanent holiday, Jake, old pal.”

Jake closed his eyes and fell asleep. By the time he woke up the next day, all the other dogs had gone to work rounding up the sheep! Well, Jake didn’t know what to do.

“You’ve been such a good dog, Jake,” said the farmer’s wife, “remember winning all those ribbons at the trials every year ‘til last? Well, now you and I are going to start up our own venture. What do you think about that?”

Jake didn’t care. So long as he was chasing something, he was happy. But do you know what he was supposed to chase __? Not the clothes flapping in the wind on the clothesline, not the cats, cows or chickens, not even the crows.

All he had to chase were the tails of nice girl dogs now visiting him on a regular basis. And he didn't even have to chase them very much!

Jake figured out what he was supposed to do pretty darn quick. They wanted him to be a daddy!

Now he was past being the best sheepdog in the whole valley, he was all set to chase the title of best stud dog in the country!

What title would you like __? How about "Best Dog in the World"? I think that suits you. What do you think? Do you want a prize __?

Barking Dog(s)

This story ends with giving your dog a treat.

Hey __ (dog's name)! It's story time! Do you want a story __? Are you ready? This is a story about three dogs - three dogs, not just one - who all loved to bark. Woof! Woof! Woof! They loved barking, didn't they __?

Boss was bass, Floss was soprano and little Sinbad barked all the notes in between. Now, Boss, Floss and Sinbad weren't related but they loved each other like family. These three noisy dogs lived with a man and a woman in a cabin in the backwoods where it was very quiet and peaceful. Except for Boss, Floss and Sinbad, of course!

The man was a cello player and the woman played the violin. Together they would entertain small groups of music lovers with exquisite adagios in diners and bars around town.

Every Sunday after a roast dinner, (Boss,

Floss and Sinbad always had some of that!) Boss, Floss and Sinbad would accompany their persons' practice sessions with some howling, woo-wooing and growly barks.

Their persons' laughter was always louder than their barking.

One particular Sunday, just before roast dinner, yum-yum __ when Boss, Floss and Sinbad were in the kitchen being very patient, there was a loud knock at the front door. (The dogs loved it when people knocked on the front door because it was their special cue to bark like crazy!)

When they saw the visitor they wished they hadn't been so enthusiastic in their welcome.

It was Mike, the big St Bernard. His person had hurt his foot while out walking and was hoping for a lift home. Boss, Floss and Sinbad did not really like Mike the St Bernard - just like sometimes you don't like another dog __. It just happens: it's a smell-thing and we can't like everyone, can we?

Boss, Floss and Sinbad gave Mike a quick, polite sniff before running back to guard the kitchen, (you can never be too careful, can you __?).

Soon the woman came in and turned off the oven - how disappointing! Then she and the man left with Mike and his person, (it was a bit tricky to get massive Mike into their little car).

They had only been gone for a few minutes when Boss, Floss and Sinbad heard a strange noise.

The glass in the back door had been broken - by a thief! Boss, Floss and Sinbad had never met bad people so they didn't realize there was anything amiss and welcomed the man climbing through the back door.

The thief bundled the cello and violin under his arms and left. What do you think of that __? What do you think the poor doggies did?

Well, naturally they just fell asleep. After all, they were exhausted by all their barking.

Soon, their persons came home and, having had a good nap, Boss, Floss and Sinbad barked and barked and barked again. This was a special treat, being able to bark another welcome.

When their persons discovered their instruments were missing, they were very worried.

They were supposed to be giving a performance that very night to some very important people. Oh no! What ever would they do __?

Later that Sunday evening, a small group of people sat in a posh cafe, quietly waiting to hear the first fine notes of a violin and the soft, even tempo of a cello.

Instead, Boss, Floss and Sinbad gave their first-ever paid public performance. It was a huge success!

And since then, the three dogs who loved to bark most in the whole world, Boss, Floss and Sinbad, toured their State and barked, howled, woo-wooed and growled to rapturous applause and, best of all - got millions of their favorite dog treats. Do you want a treat __?

Precious Dog

This story ends with some kind of gift for your dog, (a new collar or leash, a new bed, toy or their favorite food or treat).

Hey __ (dog's name)! It's story time! Do you want a story __? Are you ready?

This is a story about a precious dog. Yes, precious, just like you __!

Now, this other precious dog lived in a luxurious apartment in New York City.

What kind of dog was he __? He was not just precious, he was a Chihuahua. Chihuahuas are very small dogs who have no idea how small they are. And they have big, brave hearts __. Do you want to know the kind of life this precious dog had __?

Well, let me tell you. His routine was this: he'd waken his person, (a woman who smelled real good) whenever he felt like it in the morning by covering her face in kisses. Do you like kisses __? They would have big kisses and cuddles for a long time before they got out of bed.

Eventually, when this precious dog felt like it, he'd just look his person in the eye and she would know it was time he had something yummy to eat. He ate the finest steak, the very best fish, uber-fancy treats from the pet store, bones – lots of bones – which he liked to pick at, and your favorite - __. His person would tuck him under her arm and take him everywhere she went - theatres, supermarkets, the movies, malls, parks, even on dates - everywhere! He loved it.

Would you like that __? Yes, you would! One day this precious dog became even more precious to his person, (I know you might think that's impossible).

They were walking down Fifth Avenue when suddenly, just as Precious Dog was kissing his person's cheek and smiling, a bad man grabbed his person's purse and ran off. Well, precious dog was not happy!

All his favorite treats were in that purse! So he did something he'd never done before.

He jumped clean out of his person's arms and took off after that man. And he caught him firmly by grabbing the leg of his pants!

He may have been tiny compared to other dogs, but he was brave and fast. The man got such a surprise he tripped and knocked himself out on the sidewalk!

As he fell, he dropped the purse and out spilled precious dog's treats - and something very shiny. This thing was the size of one of his treats but it sparkled in the sunlight. Do you know what it was __?

It was a diamond. The precious dog's person had been on her way to Tiffany's to have it set in a new ring. It was worth millions and billions of bones and treats __!

Precious dog's person was so grateful she dribbled out of her eyes! She decided right there __ that she would have the diamond set into a magnificent new collar for her precious dog, instead of another ring for herself.

Now, I would like to tell you __ that you are even more precious to me than this precious dog I have told you about.

And even though you might not ever have a diamond collar, you, __ are more precious than diamonds to me. You are love itself and I will always adore you. I am so very glad you share my life. Thank you __. Do you want a gift __?

Clever Dog

This story ends with you and your dog playing hide & seek.

Hey __ (dog's name)! It's story time! Do you want a story __? Are you ready?

You know that I think you're a very clever dog __? Yes. Well, I'm going to tell you about another clever dog.

This dog was named after a very famous dog called Balto, a Siberian Husky - but that's another story.

This Balto I'm telling you about was very, very good at solving problems as Siberian Huskies are by nature.

He figured out how to get ice cubes out of the refrigerator on hot days.

He knew how to turn on the television and watch it while his people were out by standing on the remote control.

He knew where to hide the socks he stole so his people would never find them.

He knew where all the nice girl dogs lived,

(but he was too busy to do anything about that __). He knew a lot of things that many dogs would like to know!

What do you know __? You know lots and lots of clever things, don't you __? What else do you think Balto was good at?

Well, he was also very good at figuring out how to escape from his yard, which is very naughty, isn't it __?

It wasn't that Balto wanted to leave his people, no, no - he just couldn't resist the mental agility of figuring out exactly how to do it.

I know you're impressed by how smart Balto was, but wait 'til you hear how clever he was at other things. Balto was so clever he had a string of letters after his name to prove it.

He had CD, CDX, AX, MX and TD

among others. These mean Obedience Companion Dog and Companion Dog Excellent and Agility Excellent, Master Agility Excellent - and best of all, Therapy Dog.

(He also had some letters in front of his name: Am CH which means American Champion. And he was a champion in every way __, like you __ - you're my champion.)

Now, as I was saying, Balto was known as a 'Therapy Dog' what do think that is __? It's a very clever dog who knows what's wrong with people and how best to make them feel better.

Balto would visit with sick children and big people and seniors in nursing homes.

And he knew exactly what would help each different person. He knew when to play with a child or lick their face so they giggled and he knew when to just lie quietly next to a tired old person's side.

He knew when to show one of his clever tricks like 'waving to his fans' and he knew when to just sit and listen to a person telling him their secrets.

He was so clever he understood every word - like you understand what I'm saying to you right now __. You are listening aren't you __? Good dog!

Obviously, he loved listening to stories like this one. You like me telling you stories don't you __?

OK, I am going to stop telling you about Balto, and you and I are going to see how clever you are __. Do you want to play a game __? It's called Hide & Seek. I will go and hide and you have to find me when I call you. Let's go play __!

Stick Dog

This story ends with you and your dog playing with a stick.

Hey __ (dog's name)! It's story time! Do you want a story __? Are you ready?

This is a story about a dog who was mad about sticks.

He really loved sticks __!

When he was a little puppy he chewed so many sticks his poop was mostly bark! And I don't mean the noise you make __.

Max loved sticks big and small. He liked them with lichen on them, bugs inside, wet ones and old dry ones. Do you like sticks __? Yes, I think you do.

Max especially loved to bring sticks inside so he could chew them in comfort - and make a big mess on the carpet. His person didn't like that very much! Do you think there might be something more exciting that playing with a stick __?

As it turned out for Max, there was. Max

had never thought about where sticks came from until one day while out in the woods, (which was his favorite place, of course) he happened to walk into a branch. When he recovered, he bit the branch in annoyance.

Well, __ now began a different sort of love affair! Max had discovered sticks that played tug! Do you like playing tug __? Max grabbed the branch stick hard in his mouth and pulled and pulled. The branch stick pulled back - and snapped! Max's person laughed at how surprised Max was. "I'll show him!" thought Max and he walked up to a bigger branch stick.

He launched himself up in the air and grabbed it hard and held on. Oops, he was hanging in the air! Max hadn't reckoned on the branch stick being stronger than he was! But he would not give it up. He hung around for quite some time holding on to the branch stick and swinging. This was fun! Yes, fun __! He swung around and around and from side to side as he tried to wrestle this prize stick away and run off with it.

Max's person tried to pull him off the branch stick but Max was locked-on. He sure could be a bit stubborn!

Max hoped the stick branch would break so he could save face. But it just kept bending instead. As he hung around clenching the branch stick with his person asking him over and over to 'drop it!' Max considered his options.

Maybe he could learn something from this situation. Maybe he could be a bit more flexible like this branch stick was being, bending with him.

Max let go. Argh! He landed with a thud

and hurt his toe. Max yelped!

So much for being flexible - now he couldn't walk without limping. Poor Max __! His person massaged his foot (after a bit of a struggle) and offered a stick as a distraction to Max.

Max hesitated.

Oh, dear __, Max couldn't help himself, he still loved sticks!

The thing is, __ when dogs or people pursue their passion, no matter how silly the passion may seem, good things happen. And for Max it meant becoming a star!

Yes, his person started filming Max hanging from branches, his new hobby, and when the videos went viral online Max became a famous stick-loving dog celebrity.

When the boss of a forestry company saw how much Max loved sticks he asked Max to star in their latest TV commercial!

You know, __ you are a star __. Yes, you are, my star. Do you want to play stick now __?

Glam Dog

This story ends with you grooming your dog or giving them a massage.

Hey __ (dog's name)! It's story time! Do you want a story __? Are you ready?

Do you know what the word 'glam' means? I know you know lots of words but this might be a new one for your vocabulary __.

'Glam' is short for glamorous. And I'm going to tell you about a very glamorous dog.

What was her name? Her name was Contessa. She was a Standard Poodle. She lived with her person and a cat whom she rarely spoke to.

Contessa was a snob! For example, __ Contessa ignored those who called her Tess. Her name was Contessa, not Tess. Never Tess.

Contessa could do various tricks such as dancing on her back legs but she only performed these tricks at parties and when she felt like it, not when she was asked to. She liked to have an audience, you see __.

Every Friday afternoon, the maid took her to the Canine Beauty Parlor. Do you know what that is __? This Parlor was a most elegant place with marble baths for washing pretty doggies and baskets of delectable nibbles all over the place.

Contessa would be bathed, massaged, clipped, blow-dried and satin ribbons would be tied in her fur.

The staff at the Canine Beauty Parlor adored Contessa. They would order glittering claw polish colours for Contessa in a never-ending quest to please her.

Contessa was treated like royalty __.

Contessa felt this was just as it should be. It so happened that one Friday as Contessa was at the Canine Beauty Parlor, standing on her grooming table waiting to be attended to, a fire broke out!

Contessa could smell the smoke and sense the fear of her attendants but she didn't know what was wrong.

Now, Contessa had been trained to stay on her grooming table no matter what. (This was not hard for Contessa because she loved all the things that happened to her on the grooming table.)

She would happily wait for hours on end on her grooming table - it was part of the process of maintaining her beauty.

Oh, dear, __! Even though everyone at the Parlor adored Contessa, they forgot all about her and there she was, on her table being so refined and waiting so patiently! All the other dogs and people had high-tailed it out of the building in a panic.

Contessa stood poised and still as ever on the grooming table as smoke filled the room, she gasped and beautiful, elegant Contessa collapsed!

But don't worry __!

A fire officer who naturally loved dogs saved Contessa from the flames and once outside the burning building, he gave Contessa CPR! He breathed gently and quickly into her nostrils and then pressed his hand against Contessa's chest and kept on until soon Contessa coughed and regained consciousness.

She was taken to the emergency room at the Vet Hospital where she was treated in the Intensive Care Unit for several days. Even Contessa had never been so well taken care of.

But Contessa had lost her silken coat, she

had lost her stunning looks, she had lost everything she had thought important.

In fact, Contessa looked frightening!

She had lacerations and burns on her face and body and singed black streaks covered her legs. People turned away in horror when they saw her.

The soft pads of her paws were calloused and burned and bandaged.

Contessa's person had bought her another designer outfit of emerald green and silver studded with sparkles to help her feel better.

But when Contessa had the new outfit on she saw that, like her own coat and painted claws, it was just something to wear and had nothing to do with who she was.

Now, __, I'm not going to tell you that Contessa changed dramatically after her near death experience.

No, she was still as wonderfully affected as ever and still loved to be fussed over with ribbons and bows.

But something had changed.

Now every other Friday instead of the Canine Beauty Parlor Contessa visited the Intensive Care Unit of the Vet Hospital.

There, gorgeously groomed by her person, she would sit in her finery and empathy giving companionship to dogs, cats and people who were scared.

Aw! Isn't she a good girl __? Do you want me to groom you / give you a massage now __?

Angel Dog

This story ends with giving your dog a treat.

Hey __ (dog's name)! It's story time! Do you want a story __? Are you ready?

Do you know __ that some dogs are angels?

They don't have wings and they aren't always beautiful and they can even be naughty but they are angels all the same. Are you an angel __?

This is a story about an angel dog. Yes, it is.

This dog didn't know he had been sent to Earth with a great purpose.

When he was still a puppy he was left at the side of a road by someone we don't want to know about __.

It wasn't this little pup's fault that he got hit by a car, was it __? But his wounds weren't serious.

The animal control man found him and

took him to The Pound.

The poor little puppy stayed there for almost a week with only his aches and pains for company.

I don't know if I should even tell you __ that there was talk of sending this angel dog over the Rainbow Bridge.

However, it so happened that this puppy was what's called a 'pure breed' dog. When the breed rescue people heard about him they went to The Pound and got him out.

They took him to a lovely vet who gently checked the angel dog's wounds. He was a very good puppy; he let the vet prod and poke him even though he was still quite bruised and sore.

It was decided that he had to be kept in a crate at a foster home for several weeks to let his fractured bones heal. The foster people loved this little pup and felt bad for him having such a difficult time when he was so young.

Little did they know that just down the street there was a little boy who knew all about being abandoned and hurt.

He too lived in a foster home. Before that, as a baby, he had been found outside a hospital.

He had been kept in hospital for some time before he was fostered by a couple who wanted to adopt him.

They loved the boy dearly and worried that he hardly ever spoke.

Well, __ , it was destiny, of course, which brought these two little boys together.

While walking to school with his foster mom, the boy saw the puppy playing with a woman in the front yard. This woman smiled at him and asked did he want to say hi to the pup? The boy nodded but said nothing, as usual.

When he had the angel dog in his arms, the two foster moms spoke in whispers then told the boy that the puppy needed a home.

The boy's eyes filled with tears, he held the puppy tighter and then he said, loud and clear, "Can we give him a home, Mom?"

From that moment on the boy talked all the time! Mostly about his puppy whom he called Halo.

The angel dog and his boy were forever blessed with lots of love and fun times. Like us __! Best of all, __, Halo got heaps of treats! Do you want a treat now __?

Cat Dog

This story ends with a cuddle.

Hey __ (dog's name)! It's story time! Do you want a story __? Are you ready?

Now, I wonder if you might love cats?

Well, this is a story about a dog who lived with not one, not two, but three cats! Can you believe that __?

This dog had never known life without cats. She had had cat friends right from when she was a baby puppy.

Of course, she had dog friends too but she also adored her cat family.

She knew to be gentle with the cats and that they would come and sleep with her.

Because she was kind to them her cats would lovingly clean her ears and that felt very nice to Missy – did I tell you this cat dog was called Missy __?

Anyway, one day Missy heard one of her dear cat friends crying out for help. Oh no!

Missy could tell from the high-pitched scream that her friend was very frightened.

She ran towards the screaming noise and saw a dog barking at her cat friend who was up a tree.

Missy chased the dog away and waited for her cat friend to jump down.

She took her time, but when Blackie the cat landed on the ground she ran up to Missy and rubbed against her in thanks before running into the house and having something to eat.

Missy sighed and lay down for a rest. Living with three cats was a lot of work __!

She was their doctor and police officer and friend and even sometimes their bed!

That's a lot of different roles isn't it __? As their doctor, she would sniff their butts several times a day.

She'd also give them a good once-over sniff, checking for any bites or scratches or anything unusual.

She would often find scratches and lumps caused by their fighting which she would bring to the attention of her person.

As their police officer Missy was especially busy.

She had to break up their bickering and fighting. Missy would go and stand between the arguing cats and would never take sides.

Her mere presence was enough to instill calm so everyone felt safe and happy.

Missy felt good looking after her cats and the cats loved Missy.

They loved Missy so much they would fight to be the one to cuddle closest to her at night.

They would also bring her presents like

mice they had caught. Missy had to pretend she liked these presents though in truth she didn't care for them.

Of course there are lots of dogs like this who live with cats but do you know what made Missy such a special cat dog, __?

It was this: when one of her cats, Apache, had four kittens, she chose to have them in Missy's bed.

Even better, Missy got to clean the little baby kittens and help raise them.

Because of her kindness to her cats, Missy was bestowed a great honor by the King of Cats who came to visit her when she was old and no longer nimble.

He offered Missy a single wish which he would grant as the magical King of Cats.

Guess what Missy wished for __? A bone? Guaranteed four hour walks every day? A squeaky toy? No __

Now that she was getting old, she wished for a puppy to help take care of her cats. She would train the puppy in the ancient art of cat and dog love.

And it wasn't long before Missy's people appeared with a little baby puppy who looked just like Missy but tiny.

Missy was so thrilled she almost forgot about her cats! Oh, I almost forgot __ is it time for a cuddle? Do you want a cuddle __?

Bone Dog

This story ends with either a walk or a nap.

Hey __ (dog's name)! It's story time! Do you want a story __? Are you ready?

OK. This is a story about a dog who loved bones. Oh, how he loved bones! He loved bones so much he would eat a bone instead of taking a walk. Imagine that __!

This dog, who loved bones of all kinds, was naturally called Bonehead.

This wasn't really such an appropriate name because he was in fact a very smart dog.

One day Bonehead was sitting on his deck eating his favorite type of bone – a raw canon bone.

He had just started to gnaw it good and hard when he noticed a shadow moving near the fence.

He turned his body and his bone away from the shadow and carried on gnawing.

Then the shadow was there again.

Bonehead moved around again.

Before long he was turning, turning away and the shadow was following, following.

Do you follow me __?

Suddenly the creeping shadow spoke – "I'll give you a squeaky toy in exchange for that bone!".

Bonehead didn't look up; he had just reached the tasty marrowbone part. "No!" he said between noisy chewing.

"What about a tug toy?" said the voice.

"No" said Bonehead.

"I'll give you a Kong toy then!" said the shadow voice.

"Go away!" said Bonehead who was getting annoyed.

He didn't like being pestered when he had a bone.

"Please" said the voice.

Was it the whine in the voice that made Bonehead stop and look? Perhaps.

Who do you think the shadow belonged to __?

Aw, it was a little dog with a dirty, matted coat. You've never had a matted coat, have you __? So you don't know just how uncomfortable that can be.

Well, Bonehead was very interested because he could now smell all sorts of adventures on this little dog.

He stood up and stretched, sniffed his bone and nuzzled it with his nose and then walked towards the little dog who was about a quarter of his size.

No, he decided he'd better take the bone with him, you just never knew who might take it. So he carried the bone towards the dirty little dog.

"Are you stupid?" said Bonehead, "What dog in his right mind would approach another dog and his bone?"

"A very hungry one" said the little dog. And sure enough, Bonehead could see the ribs of the little dog and there was a hanging cavern where his tummy should be. Bonehead felt sorry for the little dog. Wouldn't you __?

"I don't want your toys" said Bonehead "I have lots of toys of my own."

"Of your own?" said the little dog "you mean you don't have to steal them?"

Bonehead was puzzled, "Steal them? Nope." he said.

A long string of drool dropped from the little dog's panting mouth.

He couldn't take his eyes off the bone.

Bonehead put the bone down and lifted his nose toward the little dog.

"Want a taste?" he said. The little dog couldn't wait, he jumped on the bone and licked and licked it. He'd never seen such a big juicy bone with loads of meat and fat on it!

Bonehead decided to mark out his territory again and peed against some trees.

He didn't notice his person watching from the window.

Bonehead's person went to the closet and found what he was looking for. He held it in his hand until the two dogs came inside through the dog door as he knew they would.

The little dog was worried and nervous when he saw the man.

"It's OK now little guy, you can stay here with us forever" said Bonehead's person as he put Bonehead's old puppy collar on the little dog. Have you got your collar on now __? Do you want to go for a walk - or would you rather have a nap __?

Tricky Dog

This story ends with teaching your dog a new trick.

Hey __ (dog's name)! It's story time! Do you want a story __? Are you ready?

This is a story about a dog who knew lots of tricks. Can you do tricks __?

This tricky dog, called Belle, knew all the usual tricks like 'sit' and 'high five' and 'crawl' and even 'bang! play dead'.

Her person had taught her how to do those things like I've taught you things __. But guess what __?

Belle had other tricks that she had made up herself.

You might know these tricks too __. One of Belle's favorite tricks was to pretend she was deaf when her person called her.

Another was to pretend she'd hurt her paw – that one always meant lots of cuddles and treats from her person.

And Belle found that if she scratched the

door and whined her person would get out of their chair and open the door so she could go out in to the garden.

You see, __, Belle had even taught her person some tricks!

Belle's doggy friends weren't impressed by her tricks – they thought she was an OTTPP – an over-the-top-person-pleaser.

But one day that all changed. Do you know why __? Let me tell you.

One day Belle was at the park with her dog friends and they were having fun running about and playing chase and tease with a stick.

Suddenly Belle's friend Spider, (isn't that a dumb name for a dog __?) disappeared! Yes. Disappeared!

One minute he was there and the next he wasn't. Belle took charge right away and raised the alarm by barking at her person. "What is it Belle?" said her person and Belle, barking, told her about Spider being missing.

Unfortunately, her person didn't understand what Belle was saying.

So Belle took off on a search.

Spider couldn't be far away.

And he wasn't.

He had fallen down a rabbit hole and was whining. Belle nearly fell down the hole too – it was only her bigness that stopped her slipping right down.

Belle, as you know, __ knew a lot of tricks and now she thought about all the tricks she knew. She had an idea.

First she barked to get her person's attention again and then sat up and 'begged' – she knew her person loved that trick. But her person just laughed. "Well done Belle!"

she shouted.

So that didn't work.

Belle thought again.

Maybe she'd save Spider herself.

She looked around and saw the stick they had all being playing with. She picked it up and took it to the hole.

She turned around until the other end of the stick was down the hole. She began tugging at it to get Spider to grab at it – he was a terrier so she knew he wouldn't be able to resist even though he was frightened.

She felt a tug on the stick and, like person fishing, she held the stick firmly between her teeth and ran backwards, yes, backwards __! Can you do that?

Spider flew out of the hole, still holding the stick in his mouth. Belle let go of her end of the stick but Spider held on to the stick for dear life, even later when his person tried to take it from him!

The other dogs stared at Belle in awe.

"Gosh, Belle, your tricks really are something after all!" said her Beagle pal, Freddy.

"We're so glad you know so many tricks" said her new Australian Shepherd friend, Moko.

"Will you teach us some tricks Belle?" all her dog pals asked.

"All dogs have their own special tricks" said Belle "but if you'd like to learn some other ones just have your person teach them to you". Do you want to learn new tricks __?

Easy tricks to learn together

- WAVE TO YOUR FANS -

If your dog knows how to shake hands, high five or give a paw then you can easily teach them how to 'wave to your fans'.

Ask your dog to do whichever one of the shake hands type tricks they already know and wave a treat about so they wave their paw trying to get it.

As they wave their paw give them the treat to reward them saying 'wave to your fans!'

- TAKE A BOW -

This is such a cool, easy trick. Your dog is standing up and you put your hand under their tummy at the same time as putting a treat on the ground in front of them and saying, 'take a bow'.

Your dog ends up with their chest and front legs on the ground and their back legs still standing straight - like a play bow - they are politely taking a bow!

- CARRY THE MAIL -

This can be a neat daily activity that makes dogs feel good because they have a job to do. When you get your mail offer your dog an envelope (one that's OK to accidentally tear or get soggy) then put it in your dog's smiling, expectant mouth, say their name and 'carry'.

If they drop the envelope they don't get a treat but when they do have them carry it until you say 'thank you' and give them a treat!

- BEG -

This trick is only appropriate for smaller, nimble dogs and others who are happy on their back legs.

Some deep-chested dogs such as Alaskan Malamutes and Boxers find it hard to balance on their back legs and this isn't such a great trick for them.

If your dog has a natural tendency to sit up on their hips then you can show them how to 'beg' by saying this word when they get up on their hips and then giving them a treat when they hold that position for a few moments.

- CRAWL -

You always see TV dogs like Lassie and Benji crawling. It is so easy to learn!

When your dog is in the 'down' or 'drop' position, put your hand gently on their back, (just to help them not stand up) and pull a treat along the ground a short distance in front of them.

Your dog will naturally crawl towards the treat. Give it to them after they crawl a few yards saying 'crawl'.

- ROLL OVER -

When your dog is lying on their side move a treat above their head in a semi-circle and say 'roll over' in a chirpy voice.

You might have to help them a little by gently lifting their front paws over so they get the idea of rolling over. However they manage to do it, say 'roll over' and reward with a treat.

- SPEAK -

Some people teach dogs that bark a lot to 'speak' so they only bark 'on command'.

The best way to teach this is for you to say 'speak' and give your dog a treat when they bark naturally.

Dogs can quickly associate the word 'speak' with barking and pretty soon they'll bark on command.

- BALANCE A TREAT -

When your dog learns to sit on command you can put a treat on their nose and say 'wait' and give the treat when the dog has balanced the treat for a moment or two working up to slightly longer times.

This is a feat of mental integrity and indicates your dog has learned suspended gratification which is amazing for a dog to do! So bravo if your dog manages it – they are a true, titled Tricky Dog!

City Dog

This story ends with either going for a swim or giving your dog a treat.

Hey __ (dog's name)! It's story time! Do you want a story __? Are you ready?

What do you think about dogs who live in the city? Do you live in the city?

City dogs are very smart dogs. They have lots of things they have to learn and know about.

As puppies lots of city dogs get to go to Puppy Kindy and sometimes Doggy Daycare and cool things like that __. They help them feel confident in the city.

As you might know __ the city is a pretty noisy place. You hear noises like car brakes screeching, children laughing, sirens blaring, store alarms going off and other dogs barking.

There is almost always a noise of some kind. Are you listening __? All right. I'm going to tell you about a dog who loved living in the city.

This dog's name was Jefferson. At the time I'm telling you about __ Jefferson was about four years old. How old are you __? You are __ years old.

Because he was a grown-up dog, Jefferson knew everything about the city.

When he got into his person's car, he could tell where they were heading by the buildings he saw outside and the noises and the smells.

There were smells like bread from the bakery, juicy meat from the butchers and all sorts of great smells from the parks.

When Jefferson went walking down city streets, (always with his person and on-leash) there was nothing he was afraid of; he'd seen it all before.

(Actually, the only thing Jeff was afraid

of was the vacuum cleaner at home. He didn't like that at all, what about you __?)

One morning his person woke up before the sun. This was very unusual __!

Jefferson got up quickly and followed his sleepy person into the kitchen for breakfast. While they were eating, Jefferson's person said, "hey, boy, today we're off on an adventure!"

What sort of adventure do you think it was __?

In the morning darkness, he and his person got in their car. Jefferson had his harness seat belt on so he felt secure and wasn't thrown about in the back of the car.

They drove and drove for hours! Jefferson watched all the things he knew slowly disappear through the window.

Hmmn.

There were fewer and fewer buildings and more and more trees. Jefferson liked this view!

It seemed like days later to Jefferson, (but it was only a few hours to a person) when the car stopped.

This city dog could not believe his eyes! What do you think he saw __?

Jefferson saw nothing - no buildings, no trees, no sidewalk!

Instead there was space, lots of space and something huge that moved with a soothing rhythm. Whoa – what was that?

His person threw open the car door and Jefferson hesitated.

He wasn't sure about the ground in this strange new place.

Where do you think he was __?

He was at the beach! Yes, the beach!

Jefferson loved the feeling of the sand under his paws. "Off you go!" yelled Jefferson's person and he was off!

He ran and ran in big circles and back and forth – all this space made him dizzy with excitement!

He was still wondering what the huge moving stuff was in the distance was when his person started running towards it!

Well, __ Jefferson trusted his person completely so although he was a bit scared he followed him and soon he was right next to the huge moving thing.

He smelled that it was salty water – miles and miles of it.

His person told him not to drink it or else he'd be sick.

Jefferson sniffed over the shells and bits of driftwood he discovered – smells he'd never imagined before! And he even dipped his feet in the water.

Jeff felt like a puppy again! It was as though he'd been waiting his whole life for this moment. Do you know why __?

Because, you see, Jeff was a Newfoundland dog and they love to swim.

Before he even knew what he was doing, he dived right in to the ocean and swam – and he discovered he was an expert swimmer!

When his person got into the water with him, Jeff swam with him and felt so happy he could have burst!

Jefferson had found his spirit in the water because, as a Newfie, the water was in his blood. Do you like swimming __? Well, we could go for a swim – or have a treat! Do you want a treat __?

Hero Dog

This story ends with playing your dog's favorite game.

Hey __ (dog's name)! It's story time! Do you want a story __? Are you ready?

I'm going to tell you a tale about a dog who was deaf. Yes, __ deaf.

Do you know what that word means? When someone is deaf, it means they can't hear anything. Can you imagine what that would be like?

This deaf dog I'm telling you about was called Lucy.

She was a lovely girl and very well behaved. You are well behaved aren't you __? Yes.

About Lucy - even though she couldn't hear any sound at all, she watched people and dogs very carefully.

She knew exactly what was going on because she could read body language even better than dogs who can hear. She even knew her name by watching the way her people moved their mouths or just she just sensed them talking to her.

Lucy would love it when she saw her friends at the dog park pretending they couldn't hear their persons calling them. You know about that don't you __? Sometimes you have selective hearing, I know it!

But Lucy didn't have a choice about whether to hear or not.

To Lucy, the world was a silent place and she was happy. Here's something you might not realize about Lucy __.

You know that your doggy senses are more sensitive than mine?

Well, Lucy's other senses were even more super-sensitive than yours! So although she couldn't hear, Lucy could sense things other dogs and people couldn't. It was because of this blessing that one day Lucy saved her whole family!

Do you want to hear what happened __?

It was in the afternoon when Lucy first felt a tremor running through the ground beneath her dainty paws.

The fine fur on the back of Lucy's neck stood on end and she felt strange trembles flow through her body.

Lucy didn't know exactly what caused all this but she did know it was something dangerous.

So she began to dance and bark and run to the front door and scratch and run back to her family and bark.

Luckily, Lucy's family had watched lots of Lassie movies so they knew Lucy was asking them to follow her.

They gathered a few things together –

food for everyone and the first aid kit plus Lucy's favorite toy; a velvet frog – and they all piled into their station wagon.

The family didn't quite know what to do next or where to go. But James, the little boy closest to Lucy, listened with his heart to Lucy and told the family they should drive that way, pointing east. So they did.

It wasn't very long before the family felt the same tremors and rumblings that Lucy had felt so many hours before.

They were amazed that their Lucy had known the earthquake was coming. But we're not surprised are we __? No way, 'cos we know how smart dogs can be.

But people need to listen, don't they __?

Lucy's family stayed overnight at a motel on the highway. When they told the person at reception, (who had a dog called Storm) that

Lucy had predicted an earthquake, he let Lucy stay in the room with her family and sent over some special chewy treats for her supper.

Lucy and her family sat down to watch the television in their motel room and would you believe what they saw __?

No, no, no, not a Lassie movie!

They saw their whole house collapsing under a mud slide! Yikes!

Lucy had saved her whole family!

Dogs do this sort of thing all the time, don't they __? Yes.

That's one reason I'm so glad you are my dog. You might not be able to predict earthquakes and tell me about it __ but you can do lots of other wonderful things can't you? Do you want to play a game now __?

Crazy Dog

This story ends with a blowing-off-steam energetic kind of game or running around.

Hey __ (dog's name)! It's story time! Do you want a story __? Are you ready?

Wait 'til you hear this story – you're not going to believe it __! This is a tale about a crazy dog.

Wow, was he ever crazy! Nobody knew why he was so insane. Some said he'd been dropped on his head, others blamed his siblings for bullying him and others still reckoned he was the victim of a puppy farm operation.

His person took this crazy dog – did I tell you his name __? It was Red.

Anyways, his person took Red to every vet in town. None of them could help. The drugs, the change of diet, the behavioral counseling – nothing worked. Red was as mad as mad could be – "always was, always will be" people said.

I don't even know if I should tell you some of the crazy things Red did __ 'cos you know, I don't want you getting any ideas about how to make me crazy...

But since you're a good dog, __ , I'll tell you some of the things. Some days Red would chase his tail for just about the whole, entire day. He couldn't help himself. It was like he got a lot of pleasure out of this tail-chasing but the sad thing was he couldn't stop and would do it 'til he fell over exhausted.

Red would sometimes get growly with his person! It was as though he wasn't Red at all and didn't recognize his person whom he loved.

Red could be such a nice dog, but sometimes he was plain insane. What about that __!

Red could be unpredictable with other dogs. Red's person had a hard time breaking up fights and trying to keep Red under control. It was very difficult, but he loved Red, what could he do?

You know what happened __? Do you think Red and his person moved away and lived in isolation?

Do you think Red's person surrendered him to the ASPCA? No way.

Red may have been crazy but he wasn't stupid and neither was his person.

Red's person just kept on trying to find an answer to Red's problem.

He'd listen to pet shows on the radio, he'd email experts, he even went to a couple of seminars on aggressive dog behavior - and ended up giving the lecturer some tips! But in the end, you guessed it, __ he found what he'd been looking for.

He found someone who knew right away that there was nothing wrong with Red's mind – Red was ill.

You might think this someone was another dog __ but no, it was a person who'd spent years and years studying dog health and helping dogs like Red. The other vets had missed what was going on with Red because it had been so tiny but this vet could see a tumor on the MRI scan.

She gave Red a concoction of medicines and she whipped that tumor out and within a month or so, life was very different.

Of course, Red was still a little crazy, but he was regular dog crazy.

He was crazy about treats and his dinner and crazy about playing with other dogs (he was no longer afraid someone might bump the bit of him that had been sore) and meeting new people.

He was crazy about sleeping on his soft bed and playing with his toys. He was crazy when it snowed and he'd dance in the snowdrifts.

You know, that's one of the things we people love about dogs like Red and like you and all dogs __ - you show us how to be ourselves, how to be a little crazy and love it.

I love you __. Do you want to act crazy for a while? Do you want to play __?

Sick Dog

This story ends with giving your dog a treat.

Hey __ (dog's name)! It's story time! Do you want a story __? Are you ready?

This is a story about a dog who became very sick. Her name was Scooter and she was only five years old when it happened.

That's not very old is it __? How old are you? You are __ years old.

Scooter was a Terrier and her favorite thing was to investigate any hole she ever saw.

It could be a hole in a wall or a hole in the ground – she couldn't help but check it out. Scooter always retrieved whatever she found in these holes – much to her person's delight. It was always funny to see what Scooter had found.

Thank goodness she never found any animals down those burrows! One day Scooter found something very dangerous.

She happily carried the tatty plastic wrapper filled with meat and powder to her person.

She held her tail proudly upright – and suddenly she fell over on her side and didn't move.

Scooter's person screamed and picked Scooter up and ran as fast as she could, clutching Scooter's limp body close.

Oh no! __ Scooter was so sick she was unconscious!

Scooter didn't remember being taken to the Emergency Room at the Vet Hospital having her stomach pumped and being hooked up to an IV line.

She didn't remember her person crying in the waiting room or the other dogs howling.

It was more than a day before Scooter opened her eyes again. She could hear her person talking to her. Her person was telling her how important Scooter was and how much she was needed. Her person told her not to leave just yet, that they still had so much to do and see together.

That's like us, isn't it __? Yes. We have lots still to do and see together and I too want you to know how much you mean to me. You've made my life so much better, so much more fun. I am so grateful to have you by my side __.

Let me tell you, __ , what happened to Scooter. Scooter got better with her person by her side. Her person gave her lots of cuddles and kisses and spoke to her as much as she could. Scooter felt better when her person talked to her.

Soon Scooter was released from the hospital and was told to take it easy at home. Scooter take things easy? No way! She couldn't do that! She had to live every moment to its fullest and have as much fun as possible. Every moment counted.

So Scooter became even more playful and even more naughty and even more of a joy to be around!

Scooter's person realized there were more activities she could do with Scooter that she hadn't thought of before. She wanted to find something for Scooter to do instead of running down holes.

The answer was obvious wasn't it __? She took Scooter to Agility Classes and Scooter wasn't too old to learn.

As you can imagine, Scooter loved running through the tunnels especially. They were her favorite part of the obstacle course.

And let me share with you __ that Scooter won quite a lot of trophies over the years.

And this wasn't because her person married one of the judges, __ , it was because Scooter was a natural winner!

You're a natural winner aren't you __? Do you want a special treat now __?

Sad Dog

This story ends with giving your dog a treat.

Hey __ (dog's name)! It's story time! Do you want a story __? Are you ready?

This is a story about a sad dog. Oh, dear, __ , a sad dog.

Gem was a very beautiful dog with a long curly coat. When she was a young puppy she had been very happy. But when she left her brothers and sisters, she became very sad. Do you know why __?

It was because even though she was beautiful and sweet, she had no person.

Yup, nobody to love or be loved by. Can you believe that __?

She had been bought for almost nothing as a gift from a puppy farm but the recipient didn't want her and she was sold on from person to person - maybe as many as five different people.

And none of them really wanted her. It is

very sad that this happens, __ but for lots of dogs it does.

You know, __ , Gem never had a bone or a walk on a leash with a person who appreciated her.

She never was given a toy or a cuddle. Nobody ever made a fuss of her or lovingly stroked her soft, curly coat. Gem started to think there was something wrong with her. (There was nothing wrong with her, of course.)

She had seen other dogs out with their people and she had seen a light shining in their eyes, which you know __ is the light of love.

So, Gem figured if she didn't have someone who loved her, she must be a dog that didn't deserve love, that maybe she had done something wrong - which wasn't true!

Oh, dear __. Isn't that a shame?

Gem found herself chained up in a cage surrounded by ferocious dogs who seemed to be both terrified and fierce at the same time.

Men would come in and bang on all the dogs cages with steel batons so that everyone growled and barked. No-one got any food for days on end.

I won't even tell you what sort of place this was __.

One day there was a huge racket of people storming in with big dogs wearing bullet-proof coats.

It was the police and they arrested the men who banged the cages.

Gem was picked up by one of the officers who tickled her under her chin and stroked her ears and held her tenderly. "It's OK now good little girl. You're safe." said the police officer as he freed Gem of the heavy chain.

"I think you are a King Charles Spaniel." said another police officer to Gem. (People were speaking kindly to her!)

"I'm going to take her home right after the vet check." he added.

So it was that Gem went to live with a boy dog just like her, another King Charles Spaniel just a year older than she was! He was like her older brother and was so happy to have a fur friend for company.

So, you guessed it, __ , Gem lived happily ever after.

You see, __ , even when things seem really sad or bad, if you hold on to the hope in your heart they really can suddenly get 100% better.

She found love like she never imagined. Dogs played with her and people stroked her soft curly coat. She was so happy __ because at last she was loved and free. Also, she got to eat lots of treats. Do you want a treat now __?

Christmas Dog

This story ends with giving your dog a gift, (maybe a new toy, new collar or leash, bed, or their favorite toy or treat).

Hey __ (dog's name)! It's story time! Do you want a story __? Are you ready?

You are such a good dog.

Do you know about Christmas __? Christmas is a special time of year when people exchange gifts and celebrate joy and happiness and family.

For dogs like you, Christmas is a magical time, not least because of the goodies you so rightly receive.

Let me tell you about a dog just like you who was called Noel.

Noel got his name because he had himself been a Christmas gift! I know that dogs and other animals should almost never be given as gifts.

But Noel was given to someone in the family who longed for a dog and had written "a dog" at the very top of her Christmas

Letter to Santa.

Every Christmas when Noel saw his family wrapping presents and writing cards and staying out late shopping, Noel thought about his second Christmas.

He remembered the huge tree that had appeared in the front room - his very first Christmas present. Noel had made sure to mark the tree so his family would know how much he liked his gift that reminded him of when he found his girl and family.

He remembered the sparkling lights hanging from the mantelpiece. And how he had thought they were toys until his family put them well out of his reach.

Naturally, he thought all the presents under the tree were for him too.

Well, __, what dog wouldn't? And so he unwrapped and played with them while his family slept. Although his family would have thought that very naughty, Noel had a very good excuse for what he had done.

Let me tell you __ what that excuse was, because I know you'll understand.

On Christmas Eve, while his family slept and Noel dreamed he was playing with his dog friend, Sophie, Noel heard someone huffing and puffing and chuckling.

He smelled an unusual mixture of lovely scents. He opened his eyes and saw a very large person stepping out of the fireplace!

This person was wearing a huge red coat and had a long white beard.

Noel watched as this giant of a man, who smelled like candy, carefully laid some boxes under the tree and - can you believe this __? - helped himself to milk and cookies from the table! Noel was too nervous to do anything and pretended he was asleep.

The very big person, (I'm sure you've already guessed it was Santa Claus himself) saw Noel and put his hand under Noel's chin and then laid a little box in front of him.

Noel could smell something irresistible in that box.

As soon as Santa disappeared back up the chimney, Noel opened his box, (none too carefully I might add). Out spilled his very favorite treats, carob-coated biscuits!

Well, of course, Noel then felt it his duty to investigate all the other brightly-wrapped boxes and packages.

But even after opening all of them he didn't find any more carob-coated biscuits!

Noel was now very tired so he fell fast asleep. Just before dawn his ears twitched as he heard tiny footsteps approaching him. It was one of Santa's elves! "I am Pet Elf" he said none too happily "And it's my job to go around the world and scold those naughty creatures like you who have interfered with Santa's presents!"

"But I didn't mean to make a mess!" said Noel who now saw paper, ribbons and presents scattered all over the floor.

"I know that" said the elf, "You all say that. But now you have to make amends."

"OK" said Noel, "What do I do?"

"You will promise to always be a good dog. And if you are a good dog Santa will bring you wonderful presents every single Christmas."

And so Noel promised, and it was an easy promise to keep, which is why Noel always got lots of gifts – and not just at Christmas.

And you are a good dog, aren't you __?

Do you want a gift now __ ?

About the Author

Flora Kennedy grew up with many different pets including a German Shepherd and five Shetland Sheepdogs. As a young adult she met her first Alaskan Malamute and soon had her own Mals as well as rescue cats. She was a member of the Northern Alaskan Malamute Club NZ involved in Showing, Sledding and other Club activities; fostering rescue Malamutes and writing and editing its *Qimmiq Tales* magazine. A professional writer in advertising and journalism Flora also worked as a volunteer for Cats Protection League, Sydney, Australia; Fund for Animals, Sydney, Australia and SPCA Auckland, New Zealand both in the Shelters and fostering animals at home.

Printed in Great Britain
by Amazon